BUY
RETΙ

MW01171262

FOR BEGINNERS

The Complete Guide on How and Where to Buy Amazon Return Pallets and Proven Ways to Make Money Selling Amazon Liquidation Pallets

Mary Festus

Copyright@2023

TABLE OF CONTENT

CHAPTER 1

INTRODUCTION

Have you been looking for a place to purchase Amazon return pallets? Those who are interested in learning more about the Amazon return pallet industry may like today's topic.

And you'll discover the secret to making a fortune off of Amazon's return pallets.

Learning how to acquire Amazon return pallets is an interesting issue to study as a small firm trying to increase inventory (or enter ecommerce).

Why? With little initial capital, you may begin making money right away.

And if you're a complete novice when it comes to Amazon return pallets, we've got the details you need:

The price of a return pallet on Amazon.com.
"Does Amazon sell return pallets on their own?"
Where may one go to shop for Amazon return merchandise?
Is there a place where Amazon liquidates items?
Beyond that, too!

Let's get going if that's okay with you.

CHAPTER 2

WHAT ARE AMAZON PALLETS

Amazon return pallets are what? Did you know that 46.25 percent of internet shoppers send back their purchases? That's a sizable chunk of all internet purchases, for sure.

This is terrible news for any merchant that relies on Internet sales to stay afloat.

Our total is based on the average performance of the 12 largest online retail markets in the world:

As can be seen from the table above, the average proportion of online returns varies widely from one nation to the next.

There are several causes for consumer product returns (and subsequent abandonment of online shopping):

The erroneous item was sent to the customer. Maybe you ordered a pink handbag, but the vendor sent you something completely different.

Products received in poor condition or that did not function as advertised.

Customer regret occurs when an item's appearance in use falls short of its online description.

The package was lacking necessary components. You would assume that a smartphone would come with a charger and earbuds if you bought it.

If the delivery is delayed, the buyer may look elsewhere to get the identical thing.

Is it possible to return a pallet to Amazon? Well, so let's pretend that your online business has generated $1,000 in sales. With the aforementioned return rate of 46.25 percent, you may expect to get returns from about 460 consumers.

The amount of returns from Amazon's millions of daily shoppers may build up fast.

As an added bonus, Amazon has a highly customer-friendly free shipping returns policy.

Where do we go from here? You may choose to do nothing and take a loss, or you can take action and retain the things that were returned.

For this reason, Amazon offers return pallets.
Amazon does not store millions of returned items, but rather sells them to liquidation businesses and other online resellers.

The term "liquidation" describes this procedure. In this approach, Amazon may recuperate its losses and get rid of stock that is too expensive to keep around.

So, Amazon return pallets are boxes or parcels containing merchandise that has been sent back to the company.

You may purchase one box, a pallet, or a truckload of Amazon return pallets. You have to weigh the costs against the benefits for your company.

There is a "estimated retail value" assigned to each pallet, and the majority of them end up in Amazon liquidation auctions.

Amazon return pallets may be purchased at a set price from certain liquidation businesses.

What could possibly be on return pallets?
I'd want to bring up the fact that with Amazon return pallets, you never know what you're going to receive.

It's possible, though unlikely, that you'll get nothing but empty boxes as Tom did in the above video.

If you do your homework, you can determine whether or not

buying pallets is worth the potential downsides.

Yet, there are situations when you can identify the brands or categories of items on Amazon return pallets before making a purchase.

Indeed, brown cardboard boxes are not the norm for Amazon's liquidation pallets. In addition, you may locate what you're looking for with the aid of manifests provided by certain businesses.

Furthermore, the condition of the goods within Amazon return pallets is irrelevant.

Items range from brand new to gently worn to salvage that can only be utilized for components. Particularly applicable to many forms of consumer electronics.

The one dissimilarity? You don't check the things before you purchase them, but you can probably predict what's on the return pallets.

This is why we warn against taking a chance on the online sale of Amazon return pallets.

Yet, if you do your research, selling liquidated goods may be a thrilling way to earn a lot of money.

The best way to find return pallets for sale is via Amazon liquidation auctions or other online liquidation markets.

CHAPTER 3

WHERE TO BUY AMAZON RETURN PALLETS

Who or what sells return pallets for Amazon?

If you think reselling Amazon return pallets is a good idea, finding reliable suppliers is essential. If not, your investment will be wasted.

Pallet purchases should be made through liquidation companies or Amazon's online auctions.

Amazon has auctions throughout the year (especially after the holidays, when customers return undesired presents in droves) to sell off the merchandise that has been returned.

With their many liquidation resale programs, Amazon sells returned pallets and excess inventory.

Amazon.com's Used & Fulfilled Service and Amazon.com's Refurbished Service are two of the company
Amazon's Closeout Store for Leftover Products

Woot is a retailer that provides things at significantly reduced prices.

In addition, there are a plethora of liquidation firms who get their pallets from Amazon and other large merchants.

With some experience, you may discover amazing prices on overstock products, whether you purchase it from Amazon or a liquidation shop.

Buying customer return pallets from Amazon and other major retailers is just one of the many alternatives made available by liquidation platforms.

Best online liquidators for purchasing Amazon pallets

The following liquidation sites are great places to begin your search for discounted goods.

Amazon's Closeout Sales
B-Stock collaborated with Amazon in 2018 to introduce Amazon Liquidation Auctions. It's one of the greatest locations

to find and purchase Amazon
surplus items.

Liquidation auctions with a
variety of items are available via
Amazon's Liquidation Auctions.
Get exactly what you're looking
for quickly thanks to the lots'
clear categorization by kind of
goods, geographic region, and
stock on hand.

Applicants from the United
States and Europe are now
being accepted by Amazon
Liquidation Auctions.

To participate in auctions, you will need a valid reseller certificate and a free B-Stock account.

However, before B-Stock can process your bids and payments, you'll need to fill out some company documentation.

When the formalities are completed, you may begin purchasing surplus goods in large quantities.

BULQ
If you're looking for a wide selection of liquidation goods, go

no further than BULQ, one of the top Amazon third-party sellers. They collaborate with a number of well-known companies, including Amazon and Groupon.

While most Amazon returns are offered via live auctions, BULQ provides a more convenient "set price" alternative for purchasing Amazon return pallets.

Once you discover a suitable Amazon pallet, all you have to do is add it to your shopping basket and pay for it. They also have applications for mobile devices so you can find Amazon refunds wherever you are.

Amazon returns may be searched for in a broad range of ways, including by product type, condition, quantity, and distribution center.

We prefer BULQ to any other liquidation firm because of the comprehensive information it provides in its product descriptions, images, and manifests.

Here's a manifest illuminating the contents of the lot as an example:

Listings examples in BULQ format
Keep in mind that you still have no idea how each item on the return pallets is doing.

They don't let you choose your shipment method, yet the whole price includes postage.

Prompt Dissolution
Do you want to find a brand or store's return pallet?

If so, Direct Liquidation is perfect for you since it allows you to search for a return pallet based on a certain brand or retail outlet.

There are a lot of returned Amazon items on the site, but you can also discover lots of used goods from other retailers including Home Depot, Lowe's, Target, and Walmart.

Direct Liquidation offers popular name brands such as Apple, Samsung, and Microsoft.

Hence, even if the goods' conditions are not guaranteed, it is fair to state that you are likely to locate high-value things.

Pallets may be sorted in a number of ways, including by kind, status, store, and price. Direct Liquidation is an online auction platform where users may purchase used Amazon return pallets.

Direct Liquidation makes it simple for retailers and wholesalers to sell off unsold stock.

888 Lots

With a history dating back more than a decade, 888 Lots is a veteran among liquidation firms.

Yet, it remains one of the most cutting-edge B2B platforms for entrepreneurs and major merchants alike.

You can get huge discounts if you buy in bulk, but even if you don't, you can still get great deals if you buy something little.

In addition, you may quickly and simply make your own unique lots and negotiate a price for the full lot instead of haggling over individual items.

You can get exactly what you need by creating a custom lot.

I think it's quite neat if you're trying to reach several demographics or testing out new things.

For US purchases of 888 Lots, a resale certificate is required. You must present a legitimate business registration for international clients.

To help you determine whether or not the products or lots are worth flipping on Amazon, they provide a profit calculator.

The size and weight of the pallet will determine how much it will cost to ship.

BlueLots is a well-known U.S.-based firm that streamlines the process of locating liquidation goods for your online or brick-and-mortar shop.

They maintain an organized database of returned pallets from major merchants like

Amazon. Filters are available to narrow down your search for the ideal Amazon return pallet.

BlueLots provides a wealth of data on return pallets, allowing you to make an educated choice.

All of the Amazon return pallets you purchase come with detailed descriptions, images, shipping information, and manifests so you know exactly what you're getting.

The website's user-friendliness and simplicity have made my

experiences with Amazon's return pallet auctions quite positive.

They also provide reasonable Amazon return policies for more expensive products from designer labels like Armani, Chanel, and more.

BoxFox BoxFox is a business-to-business liquidation auction platform that facilitates the acquisition of new goods and the disposal of obsolete stock.

BoxFox's no-returns policy is fantastic. They exclusively offer surplus inventory from major retailers like Amazon and others.

Your pallet's contents will arrive in pristine condition, guaranteed. Everything we send your way is completely new.

It's totally free to sign up for the site, and they even offer a mobile app so you can keep tabs on live auctions on the go.

A 7% processing charge and shipping fees are added to the final price.

CHAPTER 4

MAKING MONEY SELLING AMAZON RETURN PALLETS

Profiting from Amazon's return policy

So, you've taken the plunge and opened up shop selling Amazon returns.

You've stocked up on cheap supplies from Amazon's clearance sales and are ready to go to work.

You know in your heart that you'll make a fortune, but you have no idea how to begin. In what ways might returned Amazon pallets be resold?

You're making things harder than it is.

Arbitrage in retailing
Retail arbitrage is the most lucrative market for selling Amazon return pallets. Here, you buy things cheaply, fix them up, and sell them on Amazon, eBay, or your own online store for a profit.

Here are two simple ways to increase your success:

One Must First Restore and Refurbish
If you want to get the most money out of your liquidated items, you should spend as much time as possible fixing them up before selling them. The trick is to make the items seem "as good as new."

Products sold at Amazon return pallet liquidation sales often include broken or missing parts or packaging.

The prices you may ask for reconditioned products will go up dramatically only by fixing minor issues like missing accessories and damaged packaging.

It's simple and inexpensive to get packing materials and other add-ons on the internet. You can find almost anything by doing a search on Google.

You might use factory plastic wrapping and simple boxes if you can't locate anything else.

Expert Tip: If any of your Amazon return pallets include things that can't be resold, consider using them as sources of replacement components.

If the thought of refurbishing gives you the willies, replacement components may be sold separately.

Second Suggestion: Group Products Together

For as long as there have been companies, product bundling has been a successful strategy. It's a safe bet that you've seen this technique in action on at

least a few different online
retailers.

A MacBook, Apple Watch, and
AirPods, for instance, would
make a fantastic combination if
the pricing were right. You may
as well include a wireless
charger while you're at it.

That way, you may recoup your
investment in the Amazon
return pallets more quickly via
their sale.

Try with different bundle sizes
and quantities; you'll figure out

what works best before the next shipment comes.

After going through your pallets, separate the items that can be resold right away from the others. Make a separate stack for used goods that are in need of repair.

Finally, have a stack of items that are more appealing as a group.

What is the cost of sending a pallet back to Amazon?
If you're starting a company, it's only natural that you're curious

about the price of Amazon return pallets.

The cost of sending back a pallet to Amazon depends on how much stuff you have and how big a pallet it is.

For instance, the cost of transporting a 200-pound pallet of auto components is likely to exceed that of transporting a 200-pound pallet of foodstuffs.

Hence, without investigation, it is quite difficult to say. In addition, most websites that sell Amazon returns do so via auctions, so the prices are always fluctuating.

But to give you an idea as a small company owner, you may expect to pay anything from $100 to $10,000 per pallet.

The costs are all over the map; I once watched Mr. Beast on YouTube unpack a $100,000 pallet.

What you're really purchasing seems to be the deciding factor.

CHAPTER 5

WHY YOU SHOULD INVEST IN AMAZON RETURN PALLETS

If you're on the fence about Amazon returns, here are a few of arguments:

You can never run out of inventory.
You may find goods in a variety of places, including overstock, Amazon returns, missing cargo, local auctions, storage units, and so on. Just be sure you go

with a trustworthy vendor. Read testimonials, but only from reputable sites.

Low initial investment Compared to dealing with merchants and wholesalers directly, the price of Amazon's return pallets is quite low. You need just a few hundred bucks to get going immediately.

Products are simple to resale. With the extra stock on hand, you may open more physical locations. You may sell in a wide variety of settings, including garage sales, flea markets, social media, your own ecommerce WordPress site, Shopify, Amazon, eBay, and resale apps like ThredUp and OfferUp. The potential is enormous.

Large margins of profit
Return pallets on Amazon sell for pennies. If you play your cards well, you can convert a modest investment of $500 into a nice $2500 profit. further restate

Narrow focus on your intended audience.
The decision is yours: Your authorized buyer may choose

items at random or you can use filters to identify items they are interested in. In addition, you may design your own individual parcels.

Conclusion

You may now purchase Amazon pallets online using the knowledge you just gained. Are you prepared to launch a profitable online store?

If that's the case, you may get your foot in the door of the e-commerce world by selling Amazon pallets. It's a good method to test the waters and earn some additional cash.

CHAPTER 6

EVERYTHING YOU NEED TO KNOW ABOUT AMAZON RETURN PALLETS

Returned products are stored on pallets that are then sent back to Amazon. They are sold sight unseen to anybody who is ready to take a huge financial risk. It's possible to make a lot of money just by fixing them up and selling them again. The more you purchase, the less each individual item costs. Products that have been returned to Amazon are sold in bulk by pallet or truckload. What's the Use of Purchasing Pallets from Amazon Returning Customers? There are a number of positive aspects to the Amazon Return Pallets program that need serious consideration. First, you won't have to shell out a ton of cash. You just need a few hundred bucks to get things rolling. A credit line could be a better option to get started with.

There is a plethora of options for reselling, including flea markets and online marketplaces like Thredup, Poshmark, OfferUp, eBay, and many more. Return pallets are a great investment for any company owner or entrepreneur looking to expand their stock. Pallets are sold in bulk, and the things on them range from apparel and electronics to health and beauty supplies.

You may focus on a narrow area if you want. If you offer in more than one category, though, you may use this to learn what your clients value most. How to Get Amazon Return Pallets in 2023: 8 Top Options In most cases, returned Amazon items end up for sale on the websites of liquidation businesses. If you go online beforehand, you can see who everyone is selling their excess inventory. Finally, under "Marketplaces" or "By Seller," choose "Amazon." Let's check out what the market's offering in terms of liquidation firms. If you're in the market for a large selection of products for your company, Amazon Liquidation Auctions (US) is an excellent place to start looking for return pallets. Pallets from this direct liquidation website are available to any legal US firm. LTLs (Less Than Truckloads) of surplus items, such as those listed below, are auctioned off to bidders in the United States. Books Clothes Food Items of electronica Accessories Footwear After registering and receiving Amazon's approval, you'll have access to bidding on and purchasing large quantities of excess product. Liquidation Pallets Purchased for Returns (UK) Amazon has enlisted B-Stock to handle the sale of its returned items in the UK. While

B-Stock has auctions in many different countries, it solely exports Amazon items to the United States and Europe. Items on each pallet are in varying states of disrepair. They may be brand new or salvaged depending on the situation. You must submit a unique application to each market since eligibility requirements differ. Each vendor has their own shipping policies and prices. Some provide free or flat-rate delivery, while still others charge per pallet. Purchasing Return Pallets from Other Online Retailers to Fulfill Amazon

Orders There are a number of other marketplaces where you may buy returned Amazon pallets. Liquidation Liquidation.com is an online retailer that specializes in selling overstock inventory from retailers like Amazon and others. Packages may be purchased by the box, pallet, or truckload. Electronics, home furnishings, clothing, machinery, computers, and automobiles are just few of the categories well-represented among the used goods for offer. Lots are auctioned off with opening bids typically set at $100. In addition, there are certain lots that may be purchased right now. You must create an account with liquidation.com before you can place bids or make purchases. Payments from clients outside the US must be made by wire transfer. Each purchase above $5,000 also need this documentation.

BULQ The American liquidation firm BULQ also works directly with merchants and vendors. As an example, consider Amazon. There are three updates every day with new products for sale. The asking price might change from vendor to vendor. There are both set pricing and auctions that last for 48 hours. If you only want to check out the clearance items, there's no need to sign up. Unfortunately, you will need to sign up for an account before you can make a purchase. All clients will also get resale certificates. Pallets and bulk orders are non-returnable and non-refundable. Only US locations are accepted for delivery, and a flat rate of $30 may be applied to select orders. Shipping fees for pallets are calculated by their weight, dimensions, and the distance from the warehouse to the delivery location.

DirectLiquidation

DirectLiquidation does a lot of business with Amazon but also partners with other large retailers such as Walmart, Home Depot, and Target. Brand and store-specific searches are available on the website. If you want to buy a pallet at auction, you'll need to create an account first. Only brand-new items on Amazon pallets are available for purchase at 888 Lots 888 Lots. You may see the product's Amazon sales rank, pictures, descriptions, condition, ASIN, and Amazon reviewer rating on their site. Estimated earnings for each product are also shown. They provide standard size bulk pallets in addition to the smaller, individual Amazon pallets. You must buy the whole pallet or SKU, but there is no minimum order size or maximum allowable price. 888 Buyers from the United States must have a resale certificate in order to purchase lots. Customers from outside the US must provide proof of legal business operation. Lots incur shipping fees of $12 per box. Shipping rates for pallets vary based on their dimensions and weight. You may choose to organize your own shipment if that's more convenient for you. BlueLots In addition to Amazon, BlueLots is a US-based business that deals in returned merchandise from other major retailers. BlueLots does not mark up any of its available lots. Instead, they generate a profit by passing the costs on to merchants. You may check out what's on sale without signing up first. You may see a subset of the available stock without registering, however. UPS, FedEx, and USPS are all viable alternatives for shipping.

Shipping rates are calculated on a pallet-by-pallet basis. The usual rate per pallet is between $300 and $400.

BoxFox BoxFox is a firm that auctions off branded pallets from merchants like Amazon's warehouse and others. You may register without cost and use a mobile app to follow the progress of live auctions.

BoxFox does not accept returns, just Amazon surplus. All of the items they offer are guaranteed to be brand new. Each item has an established appraisal value, although purchasers are free to offer more or less than that amount. How to Find the Best Used Items on Amazon Buying the pallet to use for returns is simple. You should now consider how to optimize your prospective earnings by upgrading the material. In most cases, the items on an Amazon pallet have not been thoroughly examined. This implies that the products may be in varying states of repair when they reach you. You'll have some properties that are ready to sell right away, and others that will need work before you can list them. Here are some ways to get the most of your Amazon Returns pallet investment.

Classify and group In order to get started,
you must first examine the contents of your pallet. It seems sense to divide the stuff into two groups. Separate products that can be sold as-is from those that may need some work before being put on the market. When perusing the goods, think about which ones would make the most sense to sell together. Repair The pallet's contents may need refurbishment or repair. This is especially common in the

electronic goods industry. Money may be saved by doing repairs and renovations on your own. Most of the time, the repairs will be rather modest, quick, and straightforward. After you're done, the goods will once again meet or exceed manufacturing standards, increasing their resale value. Taking parts from one defective model and applying them to another may be possible if your pallets include many identical models. If a product breaks and you can't fix it, don't throw it away just yet; you never know when you may need a replacement part. Choose Out Necessary Add-Ons The absence of necessary extras like headphones or chargers is a typical cause for product returns. These kinds of add-ons may usually be replaced quickly and cheaply. A product's worth increases and its asking price rises if it can be sold with all of its components. Repack As the packaging a product is supplied in is sometimes damaged, you may need to repackage some of the pieces. Get your hands on the manufacturer's new packing or repack the merchandise if you can. A product's perceived worth might be affected by how it's packed. Did you know that 67 percent of shoppers in the United States believe that products with paper and cardboard packaging are more appealing to buy? If you can't find the original packing, use something of high quality and cleanliness that is also plain if you must use anything else. Inspect Every of your items need to go through a thorough inspection. Products promoted for resale must also be graded. It's important that the things you sell fall into one of these groups: Unopened from the factory: This is a brand-new item that has never been opened. The item is brand new, unused, and sealed in its original packaging from the manufacturer.

The box, however, has been cracked open. As part of the refurbishment process, a product is examined, fixed (if required), outfitted with any additional components, and packed. A used item has been previously owned and is fully functional, although it may have cosmetic flaws such as dents or scratches. Finally, if you're reselling anything, you should get rid of the original manufacturer's warranty. The warranty cards should be taken out of the items and thrown away since the warranties have expired. Can You Make a Profit Trading Used Amazon Pallets? That, my friend, is the proverbial million-dollar question. You can earn money, but how much you make is up to you and how hard you work. You should be able to make a reasonable profit if you carefully repair, accessorize, bundle, and repackage products. But, before buying any Amazon return pallets, you should do some homework. Finally, research each item's current selling price (if it is listed) on online marketplaces like eBay and Amazon. Think about how much you'd have to pay to replace each item on the pallet if you sold it individually. Don't forget to factor in the weight of any damaged goods. Conclusion It's exciting and entertaining to make a profit using Amazon's return policy. The best part is that you don't need a huge storage facility. Most of the items on the pallet may be returned to Amazon's warehouses and sold again. You might also try selling them on the website eBay. You don't need a ton of money or technical know-how to get going. You are well on your way now that you know where to get Amazon clearance pallets.

THE END

Made in the USA
Columbia, SC
17 June 2025